NOMADOLOGIES

NOMADOLOGIES

POEMS

Erdağ Göknar

TURTLE POINT PRESS

BROOKLYN, NEW YORK

Requests for permission to make copies of any part of the work should be
sent to:
Turtle Point Press
208 Java Street, 5th Floor
Brooklyn, NY 11222
www.turtlepointpress.com

Library of Congress Cataloging-in-Publication Data is available from the
publisher upon request

Design by Phil Kovacevich
Cover photograph of Mithat İli (center) courtesy of the author

ISBN: 978-1-933527-87-1
Printed in the United States of America

*In memory of my parents
and for Banu, Levent & Mavi*

With special thanks to miriam cooke and Bruce Lawrence

TABLE OF CONTENTS

PART III: NOMADOLOGIES

EXTRACTS

1.

I'd say we're a people of exile. A people cultivated by distance.
(Ahmet Hamdi Tanpınar, *A Mind at Peace*, 1949)

2.

The nomads have a vague, literally vagabond "monotheism," and content themselves with that, and with their ambulant fires. There is among the nomads a sense of the absolute, but a singularly atheistic one.
(Deleuze and Guattari, *A Thousand Plateaus*, 1986)

3.

There are towe sortes of Turkes, the naturall & the renagadoe.
(Sir Thomas Sherley, *Discours of the Turkes*, 1607)

NOMADOLOGIES

Part I: The Silence between Words Is Sacred

The Unjoined

You appear
        like the lurching
divinity of Christ
      (*god*-man
    god-man)
        like the Koranic
   word
       which reveals
a dilemma:
       Is it material or
mystical – poetic
      inspiration
   or divine
      revelation?
29 surahs begin
      with scribal letters
  ciphers or *sirr*s
       dropped by Gabriel
  occult and
      nonsignifying
huruf muqatta'at
     figurae
"unjoined letters"
      constellations
some say divine
      attributes, others
an ordering system
     some, initials of scribes
others, abjad 19:
     oneness.
These are the signs
     elemental particles
an initial state

of godlessness

and immanence

a silent invitation –

just as the words

of witness

begin with denial:

la illahe

"there is no god"

the letters pose

a challenge:

embrace

a material silence

or recite –

İbrahim/Abraham

الر - *elif lam ra*

Lost at sea
Mehmed Ali Kaptan
washed ashore along the
Black Sea coast of Anatolia.
                Nobody
knew from where. Eventually
he returned to a watery grave.
His father was Mustafa Çavuş
of whom nothing is known,
except he died at sea (*çavuş*
is an Ottoman military
rank).
       Mehmed is Turkish
for the Prophet.
         The son
of M-H-M-D, İbrahim, was
called "Lord" after he made
his fortune in lumber, milling
Turkish firs, that is *göknar*
trees. During the Kemalist
cultural revolution, in 1934,
this became the family name.
             İbrahim
had earned enough, making the
right contacts at Yıldız and
Dolmabahçe, to pay the
                bridewealth
of an Abkhaz from the palace
retinue, Neşeriz, whom the
relatives would call *saraylı*.

Seaborne
and Muslim, he prayed whenever
he passed the spot where his father
had succumbed to black waves.
İbrahim's son, my father,
prayed with him.
You said
that before you were ten
you'd prayed at all the Ottoman
imperial mosques in Istanbul.
İbrahim lost
all he had, except his wife,
seven kids and the old wooden
Ottoman-style house in Istanbul
overlooking the Bosphorus, where
my baba slept on the top floor
balcony, Asia in the distance.
Pointing
to the Galata Tower, İbrahim
said, "I fell from there" –
emphasizing the fact to my
father, who never forgot
anything – as they stood
in *Kismet,* the unsteady
pistachio-hulled boat
listing in the Golden Horn.
You are
a descendant of Abraham, who
tried to kill his son, repeatedly.
You Ishmael, you exile, you
iconoclast, you Rostam, you
anti-Oedipus.

You buried
İbrahim in Eyüp, among Black
Sea tombs, near your sister
who died of tuberculosis on
Heybeli, whose grave is now lost.
                    You left
your country, destroying the
idols of the Kaaba; and of
Abraham, you said, he never
complained, no matter how
brutal the seafaring became.

Ulviye Pours Water

م ل ١ - *elif lam mim*

                In the
            mosquito-heat
                of an Istanbul
                    summer, Ulviye
                        finds me in the
                            kitchen and cackles,
                                tongue loose in her
                                    open mouth; I'm
                                        a nine-year-old
                                        "Johnny" doing
                                        dishes in a sink
                                    of sudsless, soapy
                                water in the small
                            apartment on
                    Kazancı
            Yokuşu –
            the
            steep
                cobble
                    street of
                        dusty
                            boys
                                kicking
                                    stray dogs
                                        with plastic
                                        sandals.
                                        I call her
                                        Anneanne,
                                            "Mother-
                                            mother," in
                                                a language
                                                I understand
                                                but do not speak
                                                well having just arrived
                                                from the suburbs to the
                                        City of Two Continents
                                        where my family
                                                resides.

Shouts
rise from
the street;
fruit and
vegetable
sellers
push
wooden
carts,
crying out
in the bright
singsong
of their trade –
Üzüm üzüm
iki gözüm . . .
Ulviye tells
me that Dede,
my grandfather,
hadn't accounted
for my mother when
he bought the small family
plot of gravesites in the huge
Zincirlikuyu cemetery of white
tombs and tall green cypresses.
She lives in an Other world
she says. My
namesake,
Dede, hair shorn
close, sits in the living
room, his mind faded from
Alzheimer's, staring intently
or stuttering. He doesn't know
me, nor does he recognize my
mother. He remembers
only one person,
for whom
he calls:
Ulvi
Ulvi
Ulvi

.

He's
terrifying,
Dede, a man
who unsettles me. He
tosses a balsa-wood-and-paper
model plane I've been making out the
window. One night, under the light of streetlamps,
I find it piece by piece, broken wings, the box,
a small tube of glue, and instructions,
on Kazancı Yokuşu, as we
return from visiting
some one,
some *thing*
Turkish.
In
broken
English,
my mother says,
"Your grandfather, he
born near Kazan in
Russia, Tataristan. His
family was religious, and his
father, imam. They line up to
kiss his hand, you know, on *bairam*
holiday. Later, Dede sent to Syria to
study in Şam – Damascus – and from
Şam he come to Istanbul. He finish
degree in physic and chemistry. At
that time, family and friend come
to Istanbul from Turkestan and
bring him gold coin and news.
Then, during First World War,
he lose contact with them, forever.
He was Uzbek and know Arabic well.
He translate the Koran to old Turkish. He
know Russian. He believe in socialism.
He give up his religion. He
see the world like
the scientist
does,
like
I do."

8

But Ulviye tells
it differently: *your*
Dede was devout his
whole life. Allah
brought us together.
I was in a play in
Konya, dressed in
the traditional outfit
of a village girl. He
saw me there. He
asked for my hand.
My mother said I
should marry him even
though he was fifteen years
older because he was alone, a
çöpsüz üzüm, *a "stemless grape,"*
I'd have no mother-in-law
to darken my days. We
married, then your
Aunt Zuhal came
into the world, then
your mother Meral . . .
Dede *translated the*
Koran from Arabic to
Turkish longhand in
black ink; he was devout
his whole life. Ulviye
prays five times a
day, palms open
to He Who Will Be
reading from the Koran
Dede had translated. "God
could be anything," I explain
to her, later, when she
visits Detroit after
Dede has died – *Allah*
rahmet eylesin, may
God rest his soul –
"God could be a pear,"
I say, and my mother
overhears, *What the boy says*
is true, she says, taking my side.

The taxi, an old Marshall Plan
Chevy, idles roughly on
the cobblestone Kazancı
Yokuşu. Neighbors
and dirty children
stare, mouths open,
imagining a place
called "America," where
people live the way they do
on TV. Eyes wide, they see
not us, but time-travelers,
spacemen. Prayer beads
hang from the rearview mirror,
jiggling with the engine. The
Anatolian doorman asks for
a pair of Levi's, and my
mother jots down his
size. She squares herself to
me: *Did you say good-bye the
way I told you to?* I've not yet
learned to lie. She sends me
against my will up the dank
oval staircase until I find
the brass nameplate on the
door: MİTHAT İLİ, CHEMIST.
I knock and Ulviye opens
the door in tears. As instructed,
I say "good-bye" – *allahısmarladık* –
and she hugs me till I'm breathless.
Dizzy with humility, I kiss her
hand and press it to my
forehead. Walking
past her I find my
grandfather sitting
silently in the living
room: now kneeling,
now kissing, now
pressing his hand,
which I could
trace to my
own, against
my brow.

We head
        toward the old
                Yeşilköy airport
                        and through the rear
                                windshield I see Ulviye's
                                        narrow arms and hands.
                                                She holds a bucket out the
                                        window and pours water
                                after us. This is custom –
                        may you travel like water –
                but it seems untranslatable
        with dissolving meaning
    like Dede sitting
  in his chair
calling out
for her
touch:
    Ulvi
        Ulvi
            Ulvi

            .

Object Lessons

1

The fawn manages
on seemingly unstable legs
sandblasted onto a semicircle
of glass. It's
        a shard of love
from my father, the gift he made for his
beloved before she became his wife. It's
        hopelessly
simple beside the dark and formless
resin sculptures lurking through-
out our suburban Detroit house.

My father does not speak outside
of well-worn stories. But
        you can read
a story of immigration in his paintings,
which cover the walls: canvases of
Turkish factories, watercolors
of the hilltops of Ankara, oils
of the Brooklyn Bridge,
New York's Chinatown (Mott Street),
and a series of Montreal trees
        changing color,
of my oldest sister
(whose polio is never evident),
of my mother (a birdcage beside her),
of me and my twin brother in a crib,
and of the lakes of southeastern Michigan
        harbors and landscapes
and lonely people in crowds. No
one looks at each other
        no one speaks.

٢

A five year old, I watch my father,
the Exalted, in our garage,
in the iciness
of winter, unroll yards of clear
thundering acetate sheet, crinkling it,
forming it inexactly to the contours
of my plastic wading pool, to a bucket,
        to the random design
of stacked red bricks. I don't
know what he's doing, but I play nearby,
staring, smelling the clear acrid resin,
and the deep
        blood-colored dyes
as he mixes in stingy amounts of hardener,
carelessly squirts small plastic vials
of concentrated dye
        permanent and dark
(the color spraying as if from a cow's udder).
His breath is uneven, the air afraid
to enter him, or once inside afraid to leave.
He keeps the colors separate and swirling,
trying for form, attempting to capture
some *thing*, his
        absorption in the task
pouring the sheer gelatinous
rainbow, now, into those
makeshift acetate molds.

I want to know what he's done; I'd like to see.

Dried, they are captured
moments of rapture,
of incommunicability,
like hunting trophies or
rare game heads, but exactly what
        the Exalted never tells –
one piece, with a metal post in it,
he stabs into the green lawn
of our backyard, and over the years,
from humid Julys to subzero Januarys,
it cracks and chips and falls apart,
and even so
        reveals nothing
of its origin
but a rusting post for memory.

۳

I dream of my
             mother as
a bird-woman
             who's escaped
I reach out my
             hand and she
does not fly
             from me
as she does
             when others
approach
             she chirps
anxiously
             and rotates
her turret-
             head away
then back
             again I
can see
             her black eyes
periods
             on whiteface
the bird-
             woman hops from
a curtain
             rod onto my
waiting
             hand but her tiny
feet have
             become
the sharp
             coarse
talons of
             a bird of prey
piercing
             my skin and
I absorb
             the pain
because
             I don't want her
to leave

۴

the Exalted asked for her hand
                        in the traditional way
on a visit to my mother's parents
                        my father's mother
Neşeriz had hoped he'd marry another woman
                                    with more money
but the Exalted is of his own mind
                        and taking along his twin
brother
        the three pay a *kız isteme* visit
                            drink Turkish coffee
eat fruit and talk about politics and the changing
                                shape of Istanbul
and judge each other each passing minute
and though Neşeriz is obliged
                    as is custom
to request the Fawn for her son
                    she doesn't do so
instead she stands to leave
                    and the confused twins
whom she'd sent to the French lyceum Galatasaray
though they had no means
                    are bound to follow her
dumbly the three leave the apartment
                            thanking and nodding
with polite smiles as they go
                    outside the Exalted fumes
his future suspended in devious hesitation
                                "You go on your way"
his brother says
        "I'll take care of it"
                        and just two of them walk
back inside to make nice on the little misunderstanding:

Allah'in emri peygamberin kavliyle

                                kızınız . . . oğlumuz . . .

"By the will of God and the word of the Prophet

                                  your daughter . . . our son . . ."

Meral – Kemal

        M. Kemal

            mükemmel

ۺ

You

work twelve-hour days and even the neighborhood kids tease me – I
am surprised to learn you spend more time at work than you do with

me

work is like your favorite game

chess

by which you prove yourself
to me over and again – when

teaching

me you'd switch sides once
you had the advantage, giving it up to win it back again, in a Turkish

object lesson

Listening to my parents
    talk as a boy I remember
        hearing a conversation
            haunting the discussion
words that concealed
                  rather than revealed
I learned to hear double
      two stories inside each one
    fragmented and inscrutable
the
    Fawn
        whispers, *Your father*
wrote a poem about Istanbul
and the Bosphorus.
        He read
it to me last night and
when he'd finished
he was nearly
crying
    she stops
and holds her
breath
    Don't
   let him
know I
said
so

.

Nomadology 1: Crossing the Desert of Lop

ق - *qaf*

Voices tell me I'll die a martyr, upside down, flayed, and shot with arrows like Saint
  Stephen.
My mother laments not having seen Turkestan, the lands of her father, whose funeral
  she couldn't attend.

In bookstores near Union Square, I study atlases and find the İli River that flows
  close to the Chinese border, east of Alma Ata, and run my hand over the page.
My grandfather stole "İli" from the map and stuck it to himself, a tracer, a last name, a
  secret beacon.

He traveled west like a nomad to the Bosphorus, to the throat of the earth.
We're made of water flowing between the back and ribs, The Night Comer states.

In his *Travels*, Marco Polo describes the perils of crossing the Desert of Lop.
New York, Istanbul, Tashkent, İli, mid-journey I'm separated from others, my
  surroundings change form.

I see friends and enemies – *Hazer'de dost gezer, ey, düşman gezer* – nomads and
  dervishes in the subway at rush hour, voices calling my name.
I follow the sounds, the screech of metal, the clash of armor, hooves beating the earth,
  but find nothing in the fog of risen sands that turns East West and North South.

In the tramp and hum of the cavalcade, I rest my tired head on the atlas as the Khan
  whispers, "Pray that you leave the great desert."
White quartz sands cover me, layer upon layer, like Time, *kefen* shrouds of muslin, İli –
  I'll find you rushing under dunes.

The City without Voice

I must whisper when I read my father's old collection of Nâzım Hikmet poems
    whose dissident pages are yellowed, brittle, and thin enough to see through

I hear another voice that I do not recognize as my own, a voice through Time
    distant and faint, which takes me to a Threshold of Memory

The Turkish meaning reaches me only through the medium of this second voice
    weak and fragmented like the halting susurrus of pages turning

I read the title poem entitled *Sesini Kaybeden Şehir*, "The City without Voice":
    Nafile/konuşmaz sesini kaybeden şehir, Futile/the city without voice won't speak

The words come to me obliquely, not quite foreign, some I know, some are just
    musical phrases, a Turkish *makam* awakening the deepest register of my soul

These poems first reached you samizdat style, pages copied and passed hand to hand,
    as their publication was prohibited; sometimes you made copies for yourself

I look around and catch sight of the silence surrounding me, dwarfing the
    present, and I know at once that the city without voice is Istanbul

Brooklyn Bridge, 1961

Only in darkness is thy shadow clear
    (Hart Crane)

By the sky and the night comer –
    this is no modernist Hart Crane,
but an immigrant's eye onto a city.
    Out of the blueblack twilight of
your nighttime painting, a nocturne,
    verdigris spills from the top of
the Empire State Building followed
    by impasto dabs of ochre,
a reflection – an echo – onto the East River.
    Here, you'd found a surrogate for the
Bosphorus, where ghostly freighters
    like this one pass. Finishing your
residency in psychiatry at Bellevue,
    you'd said you were shocked at how
Blacks were treated in America.
    You crossed this bridge every day.
A flâneur, you walked through New York
    like you roamed Istanbul, painting
illuminated cityscapes as your
    Impressionist doppelgänger –
Times Square and Chinatown's Mott Street –
    a stranger on the outside looking in
you appeared like a city in the night
    and then you became the darkness.

The Unseen (*Ghayb*)

ن - *nun*

These are the tidings of the unseen:
Translating sacred texts was sacrilege to some
                                    to you it was the task of a modernizer.

My grandfather from Kazan translated the Koran
                                    in black ink
            from Arabic to old Turkish script.

            In a revealing photo you wear a high kalpak
walking on water
                accompanied by two figures in fezes.

Though Allah does not signify
                    you claimed that the Word of God had been
    distorted and misinterpreted
                    finishing the translation longhand in 1955.

                            Twenty-six years after the alphabet change
Dede preferred writing in Ottoman script
                            to Latin letters.

            Mismatched pages under black
                            dust rest in your empty Istanbul apartment
        along with a Victrola and Zeki Müren's
                            "Stars Wandering Alone in the Sky."

One day in hard rain I go

                      briefcase-in-hand and gather those hundreds

    and hundreds of unread

                  untouched pages from the highest shelf.

                    You had no blood relatives

at your funeral in Zincirlikuyu;

                    the stark solitude of your exile overwhelms

          me –

             heir to blasphemies of

     translation

             from the unseen.

Elegy for Baba; or, *Fenâ* and *Bekâ*

Hüvelbaki – "the One abides"

  1. *Fenâ* (Annihilation)

You were born محمد كمالدين in 1344.
                              But
became Mehmet Kemal né 1925
                    after the alphabet reform. You
believed in this secular revision
                    like many. We
were there with you, in the last days of your life
                              when
you fought, out of reflex, perhaps
                    and I saw what you might
have been as a teenager wronged by circumstance
                              by people and poverty.
You didn't trust anyone, but you accepted obligations and fate.
                                        You
didn't much like this injustice of Death
                              so you tried to leave
which wasn't a solution this time. Anyway
                              they wouldn't let you go.
The doctor said you were a frail man
                    you didn't much like him either.
Before you retired
          you might have dismissed him as "schizoid."
(and I thought cynically, in my youth
                    if I couldn't find you at home
I could always find you in the *DSM-IV*).

You came and went like the tide; we watched you like beachcombers, tourists.

You were a workaholic immigrant success

                                            with a US patent for mapping

psychotherapeutic progress.

                         Despite all, now, you'd become a foreigner

in a Florida hospital.

               We kissed your hand.

You were unsettling, a wounded bird of prey confined to a cage.

Coming to life like Lazarus

                    "Raise me up!" you said

then, "Lower me down!"

                and we did so as if you were the

                                mainmast

of the Lightning sailboat in Pontiac Lake in 1978.

                         You said

"We won't be able to see our way out of this."

                     You said

"I've seen the view . . . it's spectacular . . ."

                 You said

"Okay . . . okay . . . okay . . . okay . . ."

               You said, "Pull the ropes . . ."

You said, "It's so very crowded . . ."

You cast off the slinking whisperers: "*Defol!*"

                       ("Be gone!").

You thanked us

        and I said

hakkımı helâl ediyorum

        (untranslatable).

                 You

sketched a circle with a line through it

                with an 'x' on either side

like a soccer field indicating the positions of the center forwards

                          apposition

an angle of repose, a parallax view, a border, a mirror, a map for crossing over.

Our tragedy had been that of Rostam

                             suddenly, it was of Oedipus

as East became West

               you transformed into another kind of stranger.

                                         You

used to say that if you slept on a problem

                       you'd awaken with the answer.

I read that as a metaphor for your death.

                    The arch

of your foot rested like polished oak on your deathbed.

                           Turning

away from your leaden

            otherworldly hands

                 returning

from your absence in the world

              to the new world

which awaited its naming

           I saw waves combing

the shore for one lost thing

           under the occluded eye of the moon.

2. Bekâ (Perseverance)

As they perform the obsequies for the funeral

                                              the body-washers continually recite

the Sübhâneke and Allahümme Barik prayers. Then

                                          you're wrapped

in whiteness. Cypress trees rise up silently

                                          like robed devotees of another order. We

brought you to the family gravesite

                                like characters in a Faulkner novel

and now we stand arm-to-arm

                                at the cemetery mosque in Zincirlikuyu. We

carry you on our shoulders.

                          The imam chants An-Nur (The Light)

from the Koran as we

                    lower you beshrouded into the grave.

God speaks in metaphors to men.

                        One

who's entered an enlightened

                    state of *fenâ*

gains awareness of the unity of existence

                              in a metaphorical death . . .

to die before one dies

                    an annihilation of ego in the Sea.

                                  You

left us in *bekâ*

                  persisting in immanence

where letters and words

                  animate and inanimate objects

exist as indices of the sacred.

                    This is an initiation into insight.

The words prepare the silence; the silence is sacred.

I, too, am part of that emptiness called God.

Rest in the light, Baba, where I can see you.

Scattering Light

I am floating amidst/A light, the bluest of the blue.
(Ahmet Hamdi Tanpınar)

You're just gesture and sound. But I can still make you disappear. You rest on the bed face down and squeal "*yat,*" Turkish for "lie down." You wait until I cover half of your body with a pillow and do the same with the other half, so you're hidden under a small triangular tent. Then I call out, "Mavi *nerede,* where's Mavi?" And this starts your feet and legs moving in anticipation, but you stay silent and secreted until I grab your torso, lifting you high out of the tumulus into the air as you scream. I twirl you around, scattering light, rolling you around my shoulders and you utter the phrase you learned in daycare, "Dat's *dayn*-gerous!" before I plop you back down on the mattress and you say: "*Ay*-gain!" We come face to face. But are we playing the same game? Or is this a now-you-see-it-now-you-don't, Freudian *fort/da* séance, a window of insight into loss and return? Before long your eyes slide to the left mischievously as you repeat, "*Ay*-gain!" but now you're preparing some kind of revenge, as you turn away from me and other things about to disappear.

PART II: FIGURES AND FRAGMENTS

The Cadaver, 1949

Blooming out of corpses
these Turks – doctors, engineers,
doctors, engineers – follow
a religion of positivism,
empiricism and scientific method.
Their professors at Istanbul
University medical school
were often German Jews
fleeing the Nazis, who educated
a generation of professional
Turks, my parents among them.
In this odd photograph, probably
taken about the time my parents
met, my father sits at the head of
a cadaver. Beside him are his best
friends, Coşkun and Ahmet,
all of them wearing white lab coats.
And though it's rather gruesome,
it is an iconic image of Turkish
modernity during the Cultural
Revolution. You were dissecting
the body of the Ottoman past to
construct a new generation of
Turks. But who was this cadaver
out of which you were building
a secular Muslim nation? (And I
recall in faint outlines the story
you once let slip about pranksters
who cut the penis off of a cadaver
and slipped it into the pocket
of a coed as a practical joke.)

Yarkent, 1329 Anno Hegirae

Robed figures with turbans and fezzes
stand side by side in a modernist Muslim
mix of scholars and imams. The photo
album, the oldest thing we own, contains
partially identified photos from a corner
of the nomadic world. Maybe it belongs
in a museum. What are my ancestors
doing here in Yarkent, along the southern
Silk Road? Today this is China; then it was
Turkestan. Three of you pose in this studio
photograph from 1911: the smallest, about 7,
Alaettin, my great uncle's son, wears an ill-
fitting Western brimmed hat of modernity.
The second, about 10, my great uncle's daughter
Halima, an earringed girl all in white, holds
a flower of commiseration. The tallest, about 14
years old, in a dark fez, is Haşim, my great uncle,
Mithat Dede's little brother, whose left middle
finger is cut off at the knuckle (a wound).
You're all wearing the same handmade black
leather boots that come to an upturned point.
The photograph is in excellent condition,
but the historical memory is faded like a
threadbare kilim. Mithat Dede was born
on the outskirts of Kazan, in a place called
Mamadiş Büyük Oşma Köyü. His mother
was named Cezille, and his father, an imam,
Ataullah. They'd line up to kiss his hand on
bairam. I can see you all in your traditional
Uzbek clothes, but you can't see me. Never
would you have imagined that a century after
this photo was taken your flesh and blood
would be speaking to you from America. A

vector of my nomadic past stretches to Yarkent
in 1329, anno hegirae, connecting unjoined lives
into an as-yet-to-be-named constellation.

A Mosque in Twilight

Miniature white dice skitter nervously across
backgammon boards. Magnolias float their citruslike
    scent. The heavy stillness of the humid air, dense
with linden, lulls you, as the sun descends toward
    Anatolia and copper light mixes into the
slow blue sea. At the foot of the mosque, they serve
    amber-hued sage tea. Street dogs sleep like rocks under
the camouflage trunk of a sprawling chinar,
    symbol of empire, resting on the cobblestones
between your wooden chair and the arched entrance to
    the House of God, whose sole minaret points
away. Ghazi Osman dreamed of a chinar,
    prophesying his dynasty. Fluty, lilting
measures of women speaking Turkish rise before
    they're drowned by the swell and tide of the ezan in
shifting light. For eighteen years the ezan was called
    in Turkish, as if its significance were in
its meaning. Perhaps the dirge of the muezzin
    draws the faithful – *Allahü ekber, Allahü ekber* –
but it's the silence between words that's sacred.

Portrait of a Chechen (Istanbul)

You bore the solemnity of a warrior in your small room in Sultan Ahmet,
an exile from a brutal war that had turned Grozny into a ghost town. We
spoke in Turkish, and you chastised me because I was with Americans
whom you dismissed as being nothing but infidels. I bought one of your
black ink on paper sketches:

           A horse galloping wildly with a Chechen rider.
This is how you supported your cause. You took pleasure in shaming me –
I wasn't Muslim enough. And after all that, as I was leaving, you asked me
to come back, to visit you.

           Outside, the ezan wafted, distorted, from the
Blue Mosque; in the silence between words an immense weight descended
on me for the Dead. I think about you when I see the booth in Üsküdar,
where they sell pamphlets on the insurgency in Chechnya and postcards of
the rebel leader Basayev, assassinated by Russians.

The Honey Collector Waters My Blood (Artvin, Turkey)

The honey collector in the Realm of Peace lovingly
fed me from various vats of viscous, amber-hued
nectar, as if to impart his wisdom or to bestow
advice. He stabbed his long knife into luminous
liquid, describing the rare qualities of each as he
did so, the altitude from which it had been collected
on the Kachkar mountains, and the types of flowers
whose pollen lent it flavor.

      Heads of state made special
orders from you, you said, as you dragged the dull
edge of the knife over my finger.

       Miraculously, what
flowed from the wound wasn't blood, but liquefied
amber. As I tasted of each, growing dizzy, you said,
"My honey, it's like nothing you've ever had. It'll cure
whatever ails you." You said, "It'll water your blood."
Turning to my tourist friends, you added, what I could
not translate: *Bunlar ne anlarlar* – "What could they
possibly understand?"

An Erzurum Landscape Watered with Blood

Clouds hang in the sky like bodies. The crowd that had come to the one-strip
airport has gone after watching the plane that brought us take wing. We
are waiting, and suddenly the airport superintendent offers both of us tea.
It's a pleasant day in August and I talk with him in Turkish about nothing
much when he brings the polite conversation to a crescendo: "Our grandfathers
watered this land with their blood," he said.

You're referring to World War I
and the Russian invasion of Eastern Anatolia and the War of Independence
that followed. The tea is amber and hot. "Our grandfathers" – I begin to
understand as if it were the dull mnemonic of a bruise – through some strange
inversion of heritage – means me. You look at me and add, "No one could take
away this land." *Watered with blood.*

What can I do but listen? Though I
might have added that invading armies aren't so apparent anymore. He refers
politely to my girlfriend as "madam." "Yes, yes," I tell him, we will be visiting
the Kachkar mountains, the Black Sea coast, etcetera. I learn that one, maybe two
planes land a day and that there's always snow atop the Palan Döken mountains
which rise in jagged edges before us. In Erzurum, the winters are fierce –
Erzurum'un kışı zorludur, balam . . . Erzurum'da kaskatı, dimdik ölür adam –
the ground freezes; but now, in August, purple wildflowers bloom.

Ethnically Cleansed Village of Stupni Do, Bosnia

The season here is changing.

The fall floats its musk again.

When the leaves yellow, they hum.

When the leaves redden, they sing.

Sometimes they wail.

The earth is freshly plowed.

The dogs and the chickens

and the sheep run free.

Villagers hide

behind trapdoors

in crawl spaces.

Bodies burn.

Crosses are cut into foreheads.

Women are shot in the face.

Bodies, scattered like leaves

bleed in the sun.

Blood waters the earth.

They collect corpses

putting them in the trunks of cars.

The UN calculates

the trajectory

of the bullets.

As a boy of ten my father

refused to go to the mosque

because he didn't understand

Arabic prayers.

He waited outside for Abraham.

I read about Stupni Do

a massacre in Bosnia-Herzegovina

where my mother sends my old clothes.

The Second Coming of Brood 19 Cicadas

A Southern gothic day in August
as profound as it is mundane.
                              Spent
cicadas with black-veined wings of
celluloid rest on the sidewalk like clues
to some hidden apocalypse.
                              The horde
lives underground for thirteen years,
and resurfaces in the Last Judgment of
a mass resurrection. Ascending by tree
and branch to survive, cicadas break out
of the sarcophagi of their bodies as the
pale prophets of Brood 19 – Marlatt the
entomologist first named them –
nineteen being abjad for *vahit*:

                              oneness.
They live for only a few weeks together
as one in the liminal state of Barzakh,
a not quite Purgatory, droning in

                              agony.
White heat. My left arm still aches days
and weeks after the tetanus shot, keeps
me awake at night, and I can't sleep for the
feel of a rusty spike lodged in my shoulder.

I wonder then, in the darkness, what is the
secret of the cicadas – their buzz and
whir descending like a continuous

                          ezan?
Another August day of heat coming from
all directions. A wasp enters a cracked
window buzzing in near-perfect
geometric designs, expecting to reach the
outside. Regularly, it lands in a kind of
confused anxiety, antennae waiving, wings
flitting, legs groping for an elusive egress.

                                I open
the door, ending its aimlessness. A shadow
descends momentarily, leaflike, but I
can't locate its source. Somewhere, silently,
Brood 19 returns to the underworld
in anticipation of the second coming.

Pleiades

the light
shifted when
    we met (1)
planetary
light bending in
the curvature
of space-
    time (2)
nothing
escaped
our naming
of the new
  world (3)
the
cadence
of your
   voice
returns me
from a distant
  moon (4)
our
lives
joined
in intricate
rotation
against
   entropy (5)

a blue
evil eye
bead and
a gold الله
circle your
neck like a
contradiction
that needs no
      resolution (6)
falling
shadows
reveal
that I'm in
an elliptical
orbit
     suspended
by the light of
your constellation –
     the moon
opening like
        an eye (7)

The Resurrection and the Life

ق ح ى ع ص - *kaf ha ya 'ayn sad*

"What kind of crucifixion is this?" I thought,
walking into the theater. The lights were
as bright as those fake Hollywood scenes of
ascension. Your arms jutted straight out
from your sides, Jesus-ess. I wore a white
disposable jumpsuit, with a mask. When my
mask slipped, someone from behind raised
it over my face so I could maintain my
persona. The table started to move about
and shadows flitted with practiced gestures;
in a corner, a device with tubes surged
with blood. "There's a lot of cord," said
the midwife. The sound I heard, the one that
annihilated me, came from elsewhere. They
held you above the green operating partition.
You were wailing, bloody, with black eyes.
You froze momentarily in the foreign air of
the world (*dünya*), arms and legs askew, still
connected to your mother. In that instant, I
tried to take a picture, which later revealed
nothing but the bright empty space through
which you'd entered the world. You were
passed from hand to hand as if in a ritual. I
followed your voice. They sprayed you clean,
swaddled and capped you. With one diminutive

hand, you held my thumb and fell asleep. The new world consisted of sound and light. And your blue hands, your cognizant blue hands.

The Sacrifice of Isaac Writ Small

ا ل م ص - *elif lam mim sad*

So many relatives are reflected in your face,
facets of an emotional world. I see, now, the
way currents of emotion shape flesh, sculpting
or cinching it into form. The first lesson: I
experience your pain as my own. After you were
circumcised – the sacrifice of Isaac writ small –
I could no longer concentrate. Did we have to
enter into this contract with the divine? Your
father became the first to let your blood be
spilled by a doctor who talked throughout the
procedure as a resident stared off absently. And
they gave you sugar for the pain; and your cries
tore at my liver. For the first time little droplets
collected on the arrows of your long eyelashes.
I could not leave the room because our blood
was everywhere. The second lesson: my selves
proliferate in your gravity. Not Isaac, Ishmael is
marked for sacrifice in Islam.

The Gathering

Now you're two, leaves are falling, and it's the worst drought in recorded
history.

You grab your ball, the one they gave you at the barber: "*baw!*"

Then you pick up a book, then a toy car, then you reach for an acorn.

You cannot carry all these things, but you know nothing of the (im)possible.

I have witnessed all of your metamorphoses; I am your testimonial; I will sing
your Song of Self to the curious, *hear ye hear ye* –

You cannot carry these objects of desire and you wear a pained expression as
you look at me, because things are beginning to drop – you have no idea why.

You cannot prevent the fall.

You test the magic of words: "*Dat!*" but the object will not come to your
scuttling hands with the occult of a word.

Your lips are downturned and wet, this is not the way your will wants to wax.

And you look at me as if I might be able to do something against the forces of
gravity.

The gathering is a ritual of word and object, the secret of which is, I collect you.

But even with your things gathered in your fingers, hands, and arms – the objects
you think mean something – as I lift you up for bed, you are not satisfied.

You are wading through moods, you are waiting patiently for a turn, you will take
your things with you into another Realm as the gathering persists: a fire truck,
a sippy cup, a toy taxi, my keys, a quarter, and a cell phone.

These are the things you have summoned to your presence: the taxi, you name
"*amumance!*" and the coin, you name "*para!*"

Your hands, impatient and frustrated, now seek your sippy cup of milk – great
pauses of breath and libation as you look into the aether – before they seek the
bareness of my arm whose skin has calmed you since you were the smallest of
presences in our midst.

In the Muslim faith we aren't fallen – we aren't a fallen people who need to atone
for sins; we aren't fallen and thus we don't apologize or confess our notsin.

Rather than unburden, we gather with crablike hands the objects of the world,
hands that hold a cell phone – "*terefone! terefone!*" – and only when the fragments
of our world are within the realm of our touch do our eyelids fall.

We do not repent for the gathering or its dissolution.

You will first be in this world with your hands.

On Translation

طس - *ta sin*

I
cut
open
every sentence
disembowel it –
         stench of offal –
and before replacing
the innards with
another logic
I stare
at the
empty
thorax
silky and pied
like mother-of-pearl
         each time
seduced
    by the possibility of
your metamorphosis.

Orientalia: An Italian in Algiers

(based on a painting by Kurt Wenner, inspired by the Rossini opera)

In this palace by the Mediterranean Sea,
at this encounter between Muslim and Christian,
the throng is divided and everyone is wide-eyed
with expectation. All stare, but no one sees. No
one speaks. The animals, muted as well, have
been depicted as quite human: The leopard
with a mannish torso, the dwarflike monkeys,
the falcon on the Sultan's shoulder with a
man's breast.
         Every figure is at once connected
(animal – Muslim – Christian – Italian – Algerian)
yet somehow, alienated. All are involved
in the coffee service: the feminine boy servant
bearing down to offer a demitasse to the Sultan
who takes the cup with the gesture of God
creating Adam. This is a painting of hands, eyes,
and gestures: the raised index finger, the look
of possessed concentration, the nervous glance
(fingers in mouth), the expression of suspicion and
lust, horror and camaraderie. Who is serving whom?
What secret is the old man whispering to the Sultan?

The Scorpion and the Nightingale (Kanlıca, Istanbul)

He is a house of books, my shy scorpion . . .
      (Brigit Pegeen Kelly, "Iskandariya")

Before
      dawn
   the
scorpion
         silently
drags its
      flaccid
         tail
            like an unmanned
                        leash –
the
      nightingale sings
                  a fugue –

Death in the Palace

Mom wasn't there, we had a sitter. You came home from work and you were distraught. Everything happened oddly, differently than expected, as if time were moving in the two-forward, one-backward step of an Ottoman military band . . . erratically, as in an emergency, but this had to do with your state of agitation. We got into the navy-blue Thunderbird and without warning you slumped over the steering wheel, sobbing. I didn't know Turkish fathers could cry. I never again witnessed such a sea of emotion: guilt, sorrow, anger.

The surge terrified us. You retold stories we'd heard about how your mother, Neşeriz – may she rest in the light – was Abkhazian, from the Caucasus, orphaned at a young age, and presented to the retinue of the Ottoman palace of Sultan Mehmed V by her aunt. Her aunt was his fourth wife, Nazperver Kadın. Accepted, she was educated there until the end of Mehmed V's reign in 1918. Then, like many women of the imperial harem offices, she was married off to a man of means.

Enter Mustafazade İbrahim (or "Lord İbrahim"), my grandfather, whose lumber business along the Black Sea, including Romania and Greece, was booming. He'd even taken out polyglot ads in French, Greek, and Turkish. She had no idea about his other children, because he'd referred to them with the word "*uşak*" which means "servant" in standard Turkish but "child" in Black Sea dialect. Instead of arriving to a house with servants, she found one full of children from other marriages.

His fortunes turned, after she'd had seven children. One died of tuberculosis at age 17. Neşeriz, having tasted something of a regal life, arranged for a visitation with Atatürk through mediaries. He now resided at Dolmabahçe (in the early 1930s), a place she knew well from her youth in the palace retinue. She asked for his intercession, relying on acquaintances whose marriages had kept them in the right circles. Her argument began with God, "*Bir düşmeyen kalkmayan Allah vardır,*" she said. "Only God is immune to the vagaries of fate." She said, "I once also lived in these apartments, but now my fortunes have turned. I have three school-age sons but cannot afford to educate them." She petitioned him, using an argument of relative circumstance, that they be admitted to the French lycée to maintain the social standing that she felt was her right. He had them enrolled in Galatasaray.

You took us to a diner on Orchard Lake Road called The Palace. The three of us sat in silence, in the intimation of a permanent change of fortune for ourselves and the world.

Fragment: The Throat of the Earth

startled

  black starlings

      cross

 from Europe to Asia

     in the wake

of a twilight ezan;

     inky

 chinar trees

    rise

as a lone fisherman's

     caïque

  is borne by

Bosphorus

  currents

The Frenectomy; or, Vampires and Turks

The periodontist, looking overly tired, was on the verge of performing a gum graft and frenectomy: sawing away a strip of my soft palate with a scalpel and cutting free the membrane under my tongue. She lied to me, telling me that it would be about as painful as burning your mouth with pizza. Who wouldn't want such a procedure? But after the needles and numbing and the operation began, I felt that I was going through a Rite of Initiation, a bloodletting. The doctor, wearing surgical rubber gloves, began cutting. I could taste the blood, lots of it, my own blood. The assistant was slow with her suction device.

The doctor withdrew a hand from my mouth slightly, spattered with droplets of my blood, and asked – to put me at ease? to make it seem like I wasn't bleeding profusely? – if I had read the bestselling vampire book set in Istanbul? "I have it," I gagged out in syllables, "on my shelf." "It would be of interest to you, with your background," she said, adding, "I couldn't finish it. I got halfway through. There's a secret, and archives and libraries, descriptions of the old city, and a mystery. It was just too long." The vampire myth is set against the background of the Turkish invasion of Europe. There is a historical fifteenth-century link between vampires and Turks and Vlad the Impaler.

I felt weak, as if on the verge of fainting. A tingling began in my intestines and forehead. I placed one foot down on the ground to try to orient myself. Vampires live off the blood and body of others, like the good doctor did, clearly, but maybe like I did as well? This was a disturbing thought, but it felt quite real. Afterward, my tongue felt loose, much looser. I had always had a tightly sutured tongue. I could barely stick it out. For days and weeks to come, when I opened my mouth to speak, blood flowed out.

Elegy for the Mechanical Turk, 1769–1854

One can envision a corresponding object to this
apparatus [the Mechanical Turk] in philosophy.
        (Walter Benjamin)

You were famous for playing chess,
an Enlightenment masterpiece,
an automaton, dressed in sable
and ermine with a handlebar mustachio.
You could move chess pieces with your left
hand – disfavored among Muslims –
indicating that something was amiss. You
shook your head and rolled your eyes
when your opponent faltered. You
had a fine, long-necked Turkish pipe.
You were the kind of Turban'd Turk
Othello had killed before later killing
himself. But you were also a pure
machine at the beginning of the machine
age, an assemblage with intricate
clockwork that held a secret *sirr*. You
had a hidden operator who worked
by the light of a single *elif*-like candle,
its heat escaping from your head.
Through an elaborate system of magnets
and concealed compartments, they operated
you as if you had volition. Occasionally,
the master of ceremonies would gaze
into a small box on your desk, as if
to control the wonder of science that
made you think. You were a subaltern
mirror of the cogito. You traveled the world.
In France you were a wonder of Turquerie,
beating such historical figures as Napoleon
(who tried to cheat) and a young Benjamin

Franklin. In America, even Poe wrote
about you, with an obsession only
a circumcised Turk could arouse. Walter
Benjamin mentioned you as an analogy
for "historical materialism" tainted
by a hidden "theology" (the ugly
puppet master kept out of sight)
in *Theses on the Philosophy of History*. You
were a marvel of Orientalism come to life
living a long eighty-five years that ended
in a museum conflagration in which you
exclaimed "*échec!*" meaning "check"
in French. Nobody knew you were speaking
Turkish, in which the same word (*eşek*)
means "donkey," an insult to your masters.
By then you were in exile in America.
Only the chessboard survived the fire.
A corresponding object to your apparatus
still exists in cultural history, but I know
it can be defeated, Efendim.

PART III: NOMADOLOGIES

Sella Turcica; or, the "Turkish Saddle"

At the base of your skull rests a curved bone that resembles a broad horse saddle with high pommel and cantle. The pituitary gland, the small organ responsible for regulating the body, rides here like a caliph. The saddle-bone was named by anatomist Spigealius in the early seventeenth century, at a time when the Ottoman Empire ruled in Central and Southeastern Europe. This is a strange but revealing intersection of the nomadic war machine and Renaissance discovery. As any autopsy will reveal, in the center of your head is a Turkish saddle of bone, a taxonomic relic of the epic encounter between the West and Islam, which continues.

Nomadology 2: Tamerlane

They arrive like destiny, without cause, without reason, without pretext . . .
   (Nietzsche, as quoted by Deleuze and Guattari)

The old man pulls away the scored cerise of a pomegranate – fruit of the Underworld –
   whose whiteness is the layer of fat beneath an animal's hide as it is skinned.
He removes the red leathery peel in quarters then breaks the fruit into sections, which
   he in turn separates, revealing the fruit's essence – myriad arils of blood.
Now, cutting a quince – the fruit of the Tree of Knowledge – in half, then
   in quarters, flaying oak-specked skin with a paring knife, removing seeds, and
   depositing an ingot of flesh.
Feeding himself now, he thinks of the small Anatolian village of Kilis near Syria, where
   he was born, where they rub newborn babies with salt to protect them.
Allah bağışlasın.

He watched the soft spot on his infant's head close – the way skulls ripen.
He had named him Timur, after the horseman khan of horsemen warriors, the
   limping nomad-king of Central Asia.
I'm named for a conqueror – like Genghis, like Attila.

He remembers the scars as he slices, hands upturned like a surgeon's, glistening.
In bushes near the elementary school bus stop, a model rocket engine exploded in
   Timur's face, red-rippled, weeping in his arms, staple-size pocks on his seven-year-old
   cheeks, nose, and forehead, the scars forming a type of Braille, waiting to be touched,
   to be read, to be translated.
My head was on fire. My eyes were blinded.

Apples, too – the Red Apple of Conquest, or *kızıl elma* – quartered and peeled, and the
   house is silent, and the bowl is full.
They would travel nearly every summer back to Istanbul.
Still seven, Timur forgot his English, the tax of crossing time zones and borders, his face
   still pink from second-degree burns, the Turkish stuck inside him or afraid to leave.
Even after returning Stateside, he had to be courted by the language, while maroon- and
   mustard-colored vinyl luggage lay scattered throughout the suburban house, holding
   silk rugs, brass urns, dried Smyrna figs, coffee, kilims, leather, and Iznik tiles.

Nomadology 3: Peripheries

Ships pass between Europe and Asia from
the Sea of Marmara to the Black Sea in Istanbul
blackness
                bows and sterns lit by fairy lights
unseen engines alive and thudding
we were always traveling
                      to places
at the edge of the everyday
                        our vision fading
one chirping summer night when we
stopped at a motel in Vancouver after driving
endlessly to enter a coffee shop
where an old lady did a crossword puzzle
without once looking up
                      no one noticed us
what was it then between us
in Portland's southwest quarter
                      looking through
a motel room window that looked onto another
where a man sat
            motionless
                  on the edge of his bed
or the friend's apartment with the occult
books and the Indonesian hand puppets staring
with the acrid smell of ash in the air
a human skull on the counter
we fled in fear
                and later still the buffalo
that blocked our way
                coarse brown tufts
shedding as the sun silently sank
in South Dakota

we were the last people alive
sleeping in the Oregon woods in the afternoon
in grassy meadows with views of barren hills
and an always rising moon
                        over the cabin
by the frozen lake under snow where at night
towering fir trees gathered like robed dervishes
of an occult order
                humming or swaying
like Sufis murmuring
                        just beyond our tongue
black hawks hunted trout from a brook
leaving stains of blood sacrifice
                                in the snow
I can still hear the crystalline Milipitas River
all around us lay fallen tree trunks
                                bleaching in the sun
revealing the secret spiral pattern of their growth
as they decayed
                at night
                        the stars burned brightly
once in a while one would fall
or disappear into the event horizon
                                of a black hole
you were running from bow to stern
from railing to railing
on the ferry in the sound
                        leaning out over the sea
like a bowsprit
                Seattle receding
                        it was then
I was sure I saw you cracking
the translucent parchment of your skin.

Nomadology 4: *Homo Secularis*

م ح - *ha mim*

Saturn, who is my mother, wouldn't have her, a plump divorcée in a black-and-
  white photograph.
My fountain pens were uncapped, their black inks drying to ash.
The engineering texts on my desk lay open, a wingspan each.
I embraced the life of the mind – languages, books, cameras.
I was an engineer, but I decided, though I'd never been faithful, never been
  to a mosque, to say a prayer.
I wanted to call to someone, to hear a phrase of belonging, *Peace be with you.*
I lit a cigarette and looked into the hot, hazy, and grainy Istanbul cityscape.
I had a childhood memory of rushing into my mother's arms, jumping into
  her arms; she hugged me and I couldn't breathe.
I wanted to read to her now, from the Koran, a leave-taking, I wanted to say,
  Relieve us of the torment.
As the colors drained from the world, my heart soared like the Simurgh,
  which I followed.

Time Moves Backward; or, the Scorpion and the Shearwater

My father nods to sleep by the wall with three plate-size mirrors from Istanbul whose faces are hidden like the pictures my grandmother turned over before she prayed. No eyes should be upon us, not even our own. We've come to an Italian neighborhood in Brooklyn to visit my sister and her month-old baby. My nephew's feet fit in the palm of my hand. My father's falling head springs back. If righted, the tain of the Ottoman mirrors might reflect our lost expressions.

I have seen the speechless couples sitting in public, maybe we've assumed this etiquette. The sleep leads my father to tobacco fields near the Black Sea, to a time when his father Abraham hadn't taken a last name. They would go to the mosque together – *babam beş vakit namaz kılardı* – and my father as a boy would wait outside as Abraham took his ablutions and prayed. Once he handed my dad his wristwatch to hold. Later, his father noticed that the hour hand, or "scorpion," and the minute hand, or "shearwater," were moving backward.

His breathing is regular and heavy, the way a long-distance swimmer might keep from being overcome by waves, eyes closed against Time, crawling toward a hoped-for destination. The breastfeeding boy cries in pain, revealing panicked eyes.

Nomadology 5: Between Troy and Gallipoli (Western Anatolia)

1.

Troy lies buried, though there are surgical
openings in the earth like graves
that hold broken urns or ewers,
or sections of stone wall which demarcate
a room, a yard, a property. I
can touch a piece of Troy, a shard
of love. You hesitate at the sloping walls
of this small city magnified through myth.
When you enter, you realize
all you have left to read are traces
of what was, or perhaps, you can excavate
further. Soon, it becomes apparent
that beneath each city-plan
(there are nine Troys) lies another.

2.

In Gallipoli, you see how the earth
is scarred with long trenches
knowing that beneath our every step
lies the bones of a pair of soldiers
locked in a perverse embrace,
pulling close, pushing away.
The trenches tell a story of world chess,
but there is nothing to die for
here on this idyllic peninsula.
At the front line, even, you can touch
your enemy's hand.

3.

This is the palimpsest of our excavation.

Odysseus's Scar

*The journey is like a silent progress through the indeterminate
and the contingent, a holding of the breath . . .*
      (Erich Auerbach, *Mimesis*)

You might find yourself in the City of Two Continents, an exile
with nothing to do but recollect and write, having left your books
and papers behind to be destroyed or burned, or if you wish,
read. It's a bittersweet asylum, like being a refugee in your own
home, with your wife and maid who no longer know you.
Neither do you have your accustomed sources of scholarship,
only your Writing-as-Myth, fed by the absolute indifference
of Istanbul, which you try not to let shock you, though you cannot
help but be disconcerted: the mysterious forms, leaden domes
(wombs?), and towering minarets (phalluses?), not just paired, as you
might have once imagined, but multiple and cascading,

                                                  the geography,
a poetry in earth, a mythical story of unrequited love: Europe
leaning down to kiss a recoiling Asia. Their lips never do meet,
and between them, water: the caesarian scar of the Bosphorus
like the unbound wound of your departure and arrival (if only
you could arrive). But you have writing, and that, like a patchwork
quilt woven of the coarsest wool, will protect you from the cold
humidity of this Abode of Histories. You're writing a myth that might
be recognized by somebody else who knew or hoped to know you
and that recognition, as with all reunions, brings a feeling approaching
sedation rather than joy. Perhaps that's what lies between these continents
and constitutes the ebb and flow of a current whose meaning can only
be understood if translated out of the darkness of an unilluminated past.
The story is predicated upon remembering the scar: You have returned
quietly as the memory of healing.

Fasa Fiso

"Fasa fiso" you said, *poppycock*
when I explained you'd had a stroke,
demonstrating on my own person
the path of the blood clot
as it might have traveled
from your heart to your head.
"Fasa fiso," you repeated.
I said, "You weren't able to talk."
You stared at me with an intent,
incredulous look that sons
and mothers share.
"But now you can talk . . .
Do you know how you got here?"
"How did I get here?"
"An ambulance brought you."
"Fasa fiso."
"Who am I?" I asked.
"Erdağ."
And then I told you about your life,
in a Pleiades-like
constellation connecting
Konya to Kastamonu,
Istanbul to New York,
Montreal to Detroit, and
Sarasota to Durham.
You looked at me doubtfully.
I told you where you had been
and what you had done.
"Fasa fiso," you said.

Steppe Whiteness

A colorless, all-color of atheism from which we shrink . . .
  (Herman Melville)

the white concrete sidewalks
of a hidden apocalypse
in the midst of unfolding
traffic lights changing
for no one
WALK signs blinking
the symbol of white
namelessness
silent houses and silent cars
silence of night and
silence between people
like a language of law
the whiteness of typing paper
smells of cut grass and gasoline
the white Chevy Monte Carlo
the glare of overexposed snapshots
drug stores in strip malls
rusting beer cans
abandoned railroad tracks
the deafening whir of cicadas
empty golf courses
the white Lincoln Continental
musty basements
white ivory piano keys
empty swings and tennis courts
the white Cadillac Eldorado
static snow of the Zenith console TV
winter snow erasing everything
the white Glastron speedboat
the blue wall-to-wall carpet
replaced one day

by white Berber carpet
the emptiness and silence
an expanse of steppe whiteness
opening to the horizon
like tundra

NOTES

PART I: THE SILENCE BETWEEN WORDS IS SACRED

"The Unjoined": One interpretation of these Koranic broken letters, which are considered to be a *sirr*, or "mystical secret," follows:

> Alif (ا): for Ana ("I am") or Allāh (same as Elif, which is the
> Turkish spelling used throughout)
> Hā (ح): for Al-Hamīd (the Praised)
> Rā (ر): for Ar-Rabb (the Lord) or a final letter abbreviation for Al
> Basīr (the Seeing)
> Sīn (س): for As-Samī' (the Hearing) or medial letter abbreviation for Al-Insān
> (Mankind)
> Sād (ص): for As-Sādiq (the Truthful)
> Tā (ط): for Al-Tāyyib (the Kind) or an exclamation equivalent to "Oh" (in dialect)
> 'Ayn (ع): for Al-'Alīm (the Knowing)
> Qāf (ق): for Al-Qādir (the Almighty)
> Kāf (ك): for Al-Kāfi (the Sufficient) or Al-Karīm (the Generous)
> Lām (ل): for Al-Latīf (the Gentle) or for Allāh (using the second letter)
> Mīm (م): for Al-'Alīm (the Knowing, using the last letter), for Al-Majīd (the
> Glorious), or for Al-Malik (the Sovereign)
> Nūn (ن): for An-Nur (the Light) or a word meaning "inkstand"; begins
> Al-Qalam ("pen") surah, evoking a divine tablet and pen
> Hā (ه): for Al-Hādīy (the Guide) or for "Mankind" (in dialect)
> Yā (ي): for Al-Yaqīn (Certainty) or an exclamation equivalent to "Oh"

Gabriel is the Angel of Revelation. Abjad numerals are numerical values given to letters of the Arabic alphabet, which correspond to various esoteric meanings. Nineteen is the abjad value of the Arabic word *wahid* (one), whose Turkish equivalent is *vahit*. For more on *sirr*, see note under "Elegy for the Mechanical Turk, 1769-1854" below.

"İbrahim/Abraham": Yıldız and Dolmabahçe are late Ottoman palaces in Istanbul. *"Saraylı"* is Turkish for "belonging to the palace household." Rostam is a reference to an Eastern hero in the *Shahnameh*, who unknowingly kills his son Sohrab. This story sits in contrast to the Western Oedipal myth in which Oedipus unknowingly kills his father. "Anti-Oedipus" both describes Rostam and evokes the eponymous book by the philosopher Gilles Deleuze and the psychoanalyst Félix Guattari.

"Ulviye Pours Water": *Üzüm üzüm iki gözüm* literally translates to "Grapes, grapes, my two eyes," where "two eyes" is a term of endearment akin to "my love."

"Object Lessons": Each section is numbered in Ottoman/Arabic. *Kız isteme* is the traditional visit by the groom's family to the bride's family to ask for her hand in marriage. *Mükemmel* means "perfected"; here, it is evoked by the combined names of my parents, Meral and Kemal.

"Nomadology 1: Crossing the Desert of Lop": The effect of the passage from Marco Polo's *Travels* is quasi-mystical. The Turkish line is from dissident and exiled poet Nâzım Hikmet, and translates as, "On the Caspian you'll encounter friends, [but] foes as well." A *kefen* is a "deathshroud."

"The City without Voice": Nâzım Hikmet spent over a decade in prison. His collected works remained unpublished until after his death, but poems were copied and distributed by his readers. *Makam* refers to a system of melodic progression in Turkish and Eastern traditional music.

"The Unseen": *Ghayb* refers to absence, what is hidden, inaccessible to the senses and to reason. In Koranic usage, *ghayb* most often stands for mystery. It can refer to the reality of the world beyond reason, which mystical gnosis experiences. The first line is from the Koran. Zeki Müren (1931-1996) was an icon of Turkish classical and popular music.

"Elegy for Baba; or, *Fenâ* and *Bekâ*": 1344 refers to the Islamic hijri calendar and 1925 to the common era. "Slinking whisperers" evokes the final surah of the Koran, entitled "Mankind," which is an invocation for protection. *Fenâ* and *Bekâ* are complementary stages of the mystical path of gnosis. My father passed away in January 2015 and was buried in a family gravesite in Zincirlikuyu, Istanbul.

"Scattering Light": "*Fort/da*" is a child's game interpreted by Freud in *Beyond the Pleasure Principle*. The reference alludes to my father's profession, psychiatry.

Part II: Figures and Fragments

"Yarkent, 1329 Anno Hegirae": Hegirae refers to the Islamic lunar calendar, beginning in 622 CE, the year of the migration of the Prophet Muhammad from Mecca to Medina, which is known as the Hijra.

"A Mosque in Twilight": "Ezan" is the Turkish word for the Muslim call to prayer, known as *adhan* in Arabic. The "muezzin" is the individual who calls the ezan, traditionally from a minaret.

"Portrait of a Chechen (Istanbul)": The Chechen independence movement of the 1990s and early 2000s was quashed by Russia in a series of brutal wars that had the effect of radicalizing secular-leaning rebels into Islamic insurgents, one of whom was Shamil Basayev (1965–2006).

"An Erzurum Landscape Watered with Blood": The Turkish line is from Nâzım Hikmet and translates as, "The Erzurum winter is brutal, my love . . . in Erzurum, a man dies upright, frozen stiff."

"Pleiades": This constellation, also called the Seven Sisters, is known as either Pervin or Ülker in Turkish. The Arabic word is "Allah."

"The Resurrection and the Life": *Dünya* literally means "nearer or nearest" and refers to this temporal realm as opposed to the life to come.

"On Translation": The poem, evoking word and flesh, was written during the time I was translating Nobel laureate Orhan Pamuk's historical novel *My Name is Red* into English. The translation was awarded the Dublin IMPAC Literary Award.

"Elegy for the Mechanical Turk, 1769-1854": *Elif* is the Turkish version of *Alif* (see note under "The Unjoined"). *Sirr* literally means "secret" and evokes the mystical notion of arcana, in the sense of a teaching or a reality hidden or kept hidden. *Sirr* also refers to the notion of a "subtle organ" or inner consciousness. One of Walter Benjamin's best-known essays is "The Task of the Translator."

"Nomadology 2: Tamerlane": *Allah bağışlasın*, said of newborns, means, "May God spare and protect," in the sense of blessing the child.

"Time Moves Backward; or, the Scorpion and the Shearwater": The Turkish phrase translates as, "My father would pray five times a day." In Turkish, *akrep* ("scorpion") is the term for the hour hand and *yelkovan* ("shearwater") is the term for the minute hand. Yelkouan shearwaters are native to the Bosphorus and fly in formation up and down the center of the straits between the Sea of Marmara and the Black Sea, just above the surface of the water.

"Odysseus's Scar": Literary critic Erich Auerbach, fleeing the Nazis, took refuge in Istanbul as an exile where he famously wrote *Mimesis* (1946) without access to primary sources. Many scholarly works address his Istanbul exile.

"*Fasa Fiso*": My mother passed away in March 2016 and was cremated in keeping with her last wishes.

"Nomadology 4: *Homo Secularis*": The Simurgh is a mythical bird in Persian literary culture. It is a winged creature with the claws of a lion, similar in shape to a peacock and large enough to carry off a whale. The Simurgh is benevolent and unambiguously female. The name literally means "thirty birds." In Farid ud-Din Attar's twelfth-century epic *The Conference of the Birds*, thirty birds set out on a quest to locate the "Simurgh" as their king, which in a reflexive revelation turns out to be them. As such, it is a symbol for God in Sufism.